# Channeling Florence Nightingale

## INTEGRITY, INSIGHT, INNOVATION

By Candy Campbell
DNP, RN, CNL, FNAP

Channeling Florence Nightingale
Integrity, Insight, Innovation

by Candy Campbell © 2019
3rd edition

Photos:  Chuck Deckert and David Urbanic

Print ISBN 13: 978-1-7338445-0-5
Print ISBN 10: 1-7338445-0-3

The eponymous solo performance script is
combined with the author's life experiences.

Quantity discounts are available:
For more information call 800-407-1688 or
email candy@candycampbell.com

Peripatetic Publishing,
a division of Peripatetic Productions, USA

# Table of Contents

# Praise for

## CHANNELING FLORENCE NIGHTINGALE

"CANDY CAMPBELL'S *Channeling Florence Nightingale: Integrity, Insight, Innovation* is an inspiring read for nurses. Campbell skillfully reminds nurses of their Nightingale legacy. She takes a deep dive into nurses' challenges in the fast-paced, chaotic healthcare arena. She shows nurses how to find their voice and identify their power and soul's purpose in serving others.

"We are also reminded to always be mindful that life and breath are found in the eternal wellsprings of steadfast love and compassion. May we as nurses and concerned citizens perpetually carry the lamps of hope—the light of life, and the beacon of health into the entire world—so that hope and healing remain our witness and legacy."

-Barbara Dossey, PhD, RN, FAAN, author of *Florence Nightingale Today: Healing, Leadership, Global Action*

"Timeless! Relevant! Kudos to Candy Campbell for bringing our Nightingale legacy home to us intriguing ways!"

-Deva-Marie Beck, PhD, RN, International Co-Director, Nightingale Initiative for Global Health.

"Candy Campbell has done an incredible job of putting herself into the mind, heart, and soul of Florence Nightingale – and thus into the profession of nursing.

*Channeling Florence Nightingale* is brilliant – intelligent, creative, and highly relevant to the world of healthcare today. We need to re-spark the spirit of Florence and by channeling her spirit; Campbell is helping to do that."

-Joe Tye, author of *The Florence Prescription: From Accountability to Ownership*

"This is a wonderful book; I loved it. I especially loved how the author found her calling to be a nurse – as a stewardess when everyone vomited. I felt I was right there – visualizing all the scenes, and an integral part of them.

"This book a must read for Nurses Day and every day."

-Sharon M Weinstein, MS, RN, CRNI, FACW, FAAN, CSP, STTI's 2015, 1st place Award Winning Author, *B is for Balance.*

"The author, having been both a professional nurse and a professional actor, deftly uses Nightingale's own words to bring nursing history alive. Her unique perspective on Nightingale helps to make this book an excellent teaching tool for nurse educators who seek to convince students of the relevance of nursing history to their own experiences as professional nurses. Nightingale's story, in addition, can be empowering to young women, and motivate them to stretch their perceived limits."

-Judith M. Wilkinson, PhD, ARNP, award-winning author of *Fundamentals of Nursing; Basic Nursing; Nursing Process;* and *Critical Thinking*

"Reading Candy Campbell's book is a fascinating and empowering adventure. Her portrayal of Florence Nightingale is ingenious and her message to nurses, inspiring!"

-Beth Boynton, MS, RN,
author of *Successful Nurse Communication: Safe Care, Healthy Workplaces, & Rewarding Careers.*

"What a wonderfully creative blend of history, innovation and reflection. In *Channeling Florence Nightingale*, Candy beautifully balances education with entertainment. Without giving away the plot, I can tell you that this account of Florence's life is like none other ever written before. I admire the author's attention to detail and pride in the nursing profession. The introspection woven into the book and the personal report of Nightingale's life certainly has me feeling fond of this nursing hero."

-Elizabeth Scala, MSN, MBA, RN,
bestselling author of *Nursing from Within*

"Candy Campbell's latest book is the perfect marriage between a historical perspective on Florence Nightingale's massive influence and the zeitgeist of 21st-century nursing.

"Ms. Campbell weaves a narrative that allows Nightingale's voice to believably emerge, while also inviting the contemporary reader to respond to Nightingale through Campbell's reflections on her own career as a nurse.

""Candy Campbell offers a true gift to the nursing profession, a gift we should accept with deeply grateful relish."

-Keith Carlson, RN, BSN, NC-BC

Author of *Savvy Networking For Nurses: Getting Connected and Staying Connected in the 21st Century*

"Like Nightingale, Candy Campbell also had *the calling*, to be a nurse. She also had *the calling* to be an entertainer, with that addicting desire to touch others' lives through performance. Lucky for us!

"This author could actually BE the Florence Nightingale of this generation. Her writing and storytelling is brilliant. I've seen the performance; you feel that you're actually in a session with Florence Nightingale! It's an epic tribute to a true hero."

-Chris Hennessy, filmmaker, motivational speaker, creator of *Touched by Hannah.*

# Dedication

To nurses everywhere, who would give just about anything to be able to sit and chat with Florence Nightingale.

## NIGHTINGALE'S THREE ESSENTIAL CHARACTERISTICS OF A GOOD NURSE:

# Integrity

# Insight

# Innovation

# Foreword

"SUPERB! WELL DONE! Interesting, thoughtful and condensed. An easy read." Those were my first reactions to this book by author, Candy Campbell.

Utilizing play script, poetry, diary, and interview, this is a rich volume for anyone interested in women's history or the history and evolution of the nursing profession. The juxtaposition of Nurse Campbell's stories during the Vietnam War and Nurse Nightingale's journals of the Crimean War will resonate with everyone working in healthcare.

At the intersection of her passion for live performance and her professional career in nursing, author/performer/nurse Campbell takes a giant leap forward, guided by her deep faith in Almighty God. Let us take one more leap and make it required reading for every hospital administrator and director of nursing.

If you need a doctor, get in line and wait your turn. But if you need an answer, ask a nurse!

Having recently gone through a horrendous experience navigating the health care system in America for an elder parent, I certainly understand and appreciate just how hard nurses have it nowadays.

Given their dedication, why is our healthcare system such a mess? It's painful (pun intended) to experience our broken system. The world's mother of nursing, Florence Nightingale, would be impressed with my *Bedside Betty* advocating for my elder parent. Miss Nightingale might also be horrified to see that even with all the technology, all the machines, all the charting, nothing has really changed.

Illness is still all about the body's natural functions to do the healing; that, and exceptional nursing care and attention.

I highly recommend this short, educational, insightful, and well-written book by my friend and colleague, Candy Campbell.

-Hester Schell, MFA, Writer/Director, Recovering academic, author of *Casting Revealed: A Guide for Film Directors.*

# Preface

## AN ACTOR PREPARES

WHAT YOU FIND HERE is an attempt to capture a rather fluid solo-show on paper. Or pixels, as the case may be.

Seriously, don't expect that if you read this and see the performance you can follow along as if it were written in stone. No. I alter the contents for every group, determined by what has happened in the news of the day or week, and my own whimsical take on the audience. The premise is such *fun!*

People often ask, *WHY* did I launch into this project in the first place?

So, let me explain: I am independently wealthy and I have nothing better to do with my life.

Kidding.

I'm a masochist.

Kidding again, but not by much.

As a classically trained actor, a history buff, a Registered Nurse for more than 30 years

(Oh, where did the time go?), and an educator, I have a particular interest in the life and times of Florence Nightingale, her influence on public health, and the nursing profession. As a woman, I am interested in learning from other women who have set out to make a difference in the world and succeeded. Furthermore, as a follower of the Judeo-Christian tradition, I am interested in how faith played a role in every aspect of her life. As a scientist, I am interested in how she found no disparity with the dual declaration of faith in God *and* science.

When I first considered embarking on the writing of such a solo show, it was because I couldn't contain my glee at having discovered such a simpatico spirit. In speaking about her to anyone who crossed my path, I realized how few people knew much about everything that she managed to accomplish in life! It became my goal to use my gifts and education to bring her to life again. My hope is that a new generation of fans could discover her and be encouraged. I hope that by speaking with this *hero of health*, you will remember that one person can absolutely change the world.

As to the timing of this book, I resisted writing about the project until now because, let's face it, writing for publication is a chore.

As for the parallel commentary, I did consider taking an easier route and publishing some of my journal pages written during the creation of various bits of the show.

However, upon closer examination, one theme emerged: Prayerful solicitations to God above to please, please, *please*, give me wisdom and guidance to do this person justice, just in case I do get to meet her someday. (In my dreams, she appears out of a mist and says, "Oh, you're the one who brought me back to life! I had such fun watching you beam me into the 21st century."

Then, I apologize for any gross misinterpretations or mistakes I'd made in doing so, and she graciously forgives me, saying, "Now, now, my dear, we mustn't take ourselves too seriously. There are far more serious battles to fight. Take those ungodly *haters*, for instance. I was just having a chat about this with Mr. Gandhi...")

But in the end, it was the fans of the solo show who convinced me that they would like to *take her home* in the form of a book. I put it off until I felt guilty for not having done it sooner. *Mea culpa.*

Now is probably a good time, to ask *your* forgiveness for any mistakes you feel I have made, characterizing an icon. (Especially, if she is *your icon*! I hope you feel I have represented this grand lady with justice.)

For those who ask how long I have been preparing the role, I say: *all my life.*

Although I didn't really begin reading Nightingale's work until I entered grad school, after my three children had grown, I dreamt of becoming a nurse at an early age, and also an actress (or *actor*, if you want to be politically correct).

*Channeling Florence Nightingale* is my third solo show. All of them share the theme of healthcare and the nursing profession.[1]

You may be surprised to learn, as was I, that Nightingale penned over 200 publications, and that over 15,000 of her personal letters are extant. At this writing, thanks to the changes brought forth by the Internet, Nightingale's works are available to anyone. I encourage you to read them.

Meanwhile, I hope you will suspend your disbelief and enjoy the premise:

If Florence Nightingale could speak to those of us in the healthcare professions today, she would have a lot to say.

# Act I Scene i

## HOW DO YOU SPELL INTEGRITY?

SCUTARI
Nov 4, 1854.
I wish you could have been there.
Three thousand injured, lying in barracks,
used as a hospital, then
With miles and miles of fallen men.
*Boys,* actually, sixteen to twenty-two year
olds---
Heroes, 'twas clear...
Ohhh. (Switch gear, switch gear)
'Twas built on a cesspool, that hell hole, *at
Scutari,*
Which contaminated the water *and* the
ground, all around.

Enter Cholera, our uninvited guest. The
pestilence *unseen,*
Who, by the time we arrived, took more than
60% of the lives.
When the wounded appeared on shore,
Caked with mud and gore,
They'd been traveling, by ship, for eight or
nine days,
Thru wind and waves,
No shoes, nor boots, all left behind,
most missing an appendage;
On the battlefield, upended

1

With their minds.
There were no beds, no furniture.
The floor---
How shall I describe it all?
Watch your step!
To fall would be *excremental* !
We dubbed it *B-M-S,* for blood, mud, and stool.


For every 95 patients there was one surgeon,
Who sawed and sawed from sun to sun,
From one mother's son to another, without a nurse.
The *orderlies* brought no order,
But thievery to the quarter.
There were no operating tables, no blankets,
No labels, no morphine.
There was chloroform, but on the norm,
'Twas rarely used.
The doctor said, "In your haste it might be wasted,"
And I replied, "Only if you hypothesize none will survive,"
"That assumption was, generally, correct."


To paraphrase a once popular song:
Mother told me not to come!
Each time I reflected on the day I made that announcement,
I *recalled* her words of wisdom...


(Florence) Mother! Have you seen in The Times today, about the Crimean Conflict?

It says here, more soldiers are dying from disease, than from wounds received in combat!

(Mother) Yes, dear. I heard. Dreadful. *Biscuit?*

(Florence) No. Mother, please, listen. Lord Herbert has asked me to supervise the very first British Army Nurse Corps, in the Turkish Military hospital.

(Mother) What?? The Minister of War wants our daughter to journey to a God-forsaken land? To do *what*?

(Florence) Why, to care for our injured soldiers, Mama!

(Mother) You'll so no such thing. William. Wake up! Did you hear what your friend, Lord Herbert has proposed?

(Father) What? Lord Herbert, proposed? But, he's already married!

(Florence) Oh, father, I'm to travel to the Ottoman Empire, as a nurse.

(Father) Preposterous! I won't have it!

(Mother) Precisely what I told her!

(Florence) Father, mother, please. I'm not a child. I'm 34 years old. And I did not intend to ask your *permission*, but your blessing!

(Father) A warning, my pet, you're still my responsibility! I won't have it, I tell you.
Wait til I give that Herbert a piece of my mind. He should have inquired of *me, first*!

But I knew what must be done.
I *would* go...
Or my name's not Flo.

Once we arrived, a most unwelcome surprise,
We were *scorned* by the physician staff,
Warned to turn around, and retreat!
We had no such intention.
We stood our ground,
(Not to mention, the journey!)
'Twas clear we were needed.
Our mission would be heeded.

"We are *nurses* with a mandate from the Army.
"Reinforcements are we!"
The patronistic view did gall me:
"Ladies have no business in the Army."
 Blimey!

An obstructionist view of women in war.
To be sure, not *unwarranted* in times past, true.
But those were women of ill repute, not me (nor you)
Given too much strong drink, were they.

How could they think our cadre
Of 18 Sisters of Mercy and 20 others,
Some old enough to be their mothers, trained
nurses,
Was the same sort? They sold us short.

So, we resolved not to argue
With disingenuous suppositions.
"Proceed until apprehended "became our
motto.
 (And I wished father were there to
 give a good set-down at such impertinence!)

SO, we camped in and proved our mettle.
Not permitted to do proper nurses' work,
We did not shirk our duties,
But started with a kettle,
In which to wash soldier's clothes!
We cast the shutters aside,
Opened windows wide
Cleansing the putrefaction inside
Bodies, minds, and hearts.
And with help from the least infirm,
Watched cockroaches squirm.
We cleaned that place with fastidious grace,
Ceiling to floor mats.
A brush in one hand, and a broom in the
other.
We scrubbed the floors and whacked the
rats!
Seriously. As Bob's your uncle!

Then, with the help of French- chef, Soyer,
We created an invalid's kitchen,
Prepared appealing meals on wheels

For patients with special dietary needs;
We made bandages and sheets
And stitched in the first I-See-You (ICU) bedshirts.
We knit stocking stump covers,
For a different sort of living fast and dying young.
'Twas no fun.
Such violence was absolutely unjustified,
But our work had begun.
We added a library and a classroom,
Quills, ink, and paper to write home.

We instituted a program of physical therapy,
While vitamin D was unknown to me,
Intuitively, seemed so natural,
To sit in sunny air, walk about, and deeply respirate.
(Research supports our patient care.)
We were making progress there.
Four months passed till we heard, thru a little bird
"Your self-respect has arrived. We are now disposed to approve
your permission to serve...as nurses."

Meanwhile, I wrote Sidney Herbert about the cesspool problem,
The news?
He dispatched two structural engineers and a hydro expert,
With views.
Men of purpose, whose attention to detail

At first denied my splendid expectations of a
hundred year old building,
But they were made manifest by running
water.
Luxury, not a fantasy
Any longer!
The death rate from disease
Lowered to two percent.
Bazonga!

'Twas odd.
The newspapers hailed *me* the instigator
who solved it?
Simply put, the staff was too over-burdened
before.
But I say,
Those engineers were also heroes of the war!

We became a *team* with a *dream.*
We dared to care.
So, we made a difference.
And that
Was Scutari.

# PERSPECTIVE ON INTEGRITY

This is Candy again. I will be chipping in my two cents after each chunk of the text to tell you what I hope you agree are interesting parallel stories related to the previous scenes.

The story of why I decided Miss Nightingale would write poetry has a practical angle.

Historically, Nightingale's first serious admirer was Moncton Milnes, Lord Houghton, who was a poet. I imagined him reading her his poems from time to time, wishing to please her. I imagined she was pleased, and that she would have quite a lot to say about each one. Based upon her copious writing, I think this is a fair assumption.

But that wasn't the real reason.

In the winter of 2012, when I first began creating the show, I had been meeting with the Creative Director, Bobby Weinapple, here in San Francisco. We had done quite a lot of contextual groundwork. We discussed the premise and what she would do, if she could return. Until then, the show was expected to be a sort of "trunk show," which included my stepping into a few other characters, using limited props, and no costumes.

That session, we loosely timed what I had written so far. It was clear that I had more than two hours of material, but I had been asked to perform for only 40-50 minutes. Decision-time! I left in a quandary.

I was on the train back to the East Bay, and a person in front of me was listening to some sort of poetry through his headphones, which was loud enough for me to hear. (Scratch that. It was loud enough for *everyone* around to hear. I was worried about his ears!) After a night of fitful sleep, trying to sort out how to shorten the show and make Miss Nightingale relevant to today, I awoke with the answer: spoken-word poetry!

(See: *Ode To The Caregiver* for the next poem that came from the same session.)

As I sat down to write, it felt as if I were channeling my hero (hence the title). The piece nearly wrote itself. When I looked up, I'd been writing for six hours. As Julia Cameron of *The Artist's Way*[2] would say, it's as if the universe opens up and just rains ideas, like sunbeams. I'm sure I couldn't catch all the sunbeams that rained down that day.

# Act II Scene ii

## INTEGRITY OF 'THE CALL'

IT HAS BEEN OVER 100 YEARS since I completed my earthly voyage. Although I always thought of myself as an aficionado of the arts (indeed, as a girl I dreamt of singing opera and dancing on the stage) alas, that was not my path.

I know what you're probably thinking:
"Why did you leave the easy, gentrified life, and travel to a faraway land in time of war, against the wishes and advice of your family and most of your friends?"

I understand that for anyone who values personal comfort over uncertain conditions, my choice may seem absurd. In fact, 'twas the spiritual battle I fought early on, knowing that to find oneself one must lose oneself.

It was a matter of faith. Yes, I was compelled to action because of: *The Call.*

Just prior to the beginning of my 17th year, I experienced what I can only describe as an extraordinary answer to prayer.

I had been pondering those universal questions: Who am I? Why am I here? I'd prayed earnestly for direction. I knew my heart's desire was to follow God and serve humankind, but how?

It took some time to sort out precisely what this calling was *to.*

I recall the first time I spoke up to my parents.

(Florence) Father, Mother, I believe God has called me to a life of public service.
I want to become...a nurse.

(Aside) You would have thought I had asked to become a scullery maid.

(Mother) *Whaaaat??*

Such drama. It was...

(Mother) Out of the question! Unthinkable! Are you ill, child? Perhaps it was the salmon cook served. I thought it was a bit sketchy.

You see, in that day, any woman of my social station was expected to marry and run the house. Noble undertakings, to be sure, for many. Well, for most, I daresay.

Unlike today, so it seems, where one navigates social status rather like a balloon. One goes up and down with the changing winds...? Curious.

However, there was little movement, then, between the classes. As a result, there were precious few professions open to women, other than the *oldest profession*, if you get my drift. Singers, dancers, actors, may have achieved some notoriety, but they did not achieve a place in gentile society.

One could ascribe to be a nun, a midwife, a wet nurse, or a governess. Those were the only respectable vocations. And only nuns, or the brethren of the church, completed bedside nursing. Others, called into service as orderlies, were in the military, or those who lived in workhouses, in exchange for meager sustenance.

Please understand. Per the law of the land, as a woman, I owned nothing and I was financially dependent upon Father. As there was no male heir for my father's estate, neither my sister nor myself would inherit it. The estate would pass to my elder sister's husband, where it remains to this day.

Said plainly, in my day, women were chattel -- beloved chattel, perhaps, but *possessions,* nevertheless. And if I were married, believe me, no husband of *that* world, would have allowed his wife to pursue a career. It was a difficult decision, but I refused the hand in marriage of my dear friend, Lord Houghton. 'Twas clear, I would live my life differently.

Worse yet, my mother and sister condemned the idea as a reprehensible assault on the family's social status, and the scandal this would cause.

"Do not serve that *dish of irresponsibility* onto my plate!" my sister said.

The inevitable controversy would fall on the family, unless I was to join a religious order, which was not my intent.

Eventually, I was *allowed* the training.
But Mother was so upset with Father, he moved into some rooms at his club, for a long time.

Mother worried, extensively, which is what mothers do, I suppose.

I had to remind her more than once:

Mother, scripture says, when God calls us to some good work, He will keep us, and preserve us, that we might accomplish it.[3] And if it is His will that my life should be cut short while so doing, so be it. You know, there is no death, only transformation.

# PERSPECTIVE ON *THE CALLING*

MANY OF US IDENTIFY MOMENTS when we knew we had a calling to healthcare professions, even if it wasn't a specific calling from God. I have heard many such stories from nurses the world over. They seem to fall into three categories:

1.Those who witnessed a family member's sickness and helped care for that person,

2. Those who were the patient, who thanked and admired the nurses who cared for you,

3.Those whose family desired for you to be a doctor, but then you realized how long it would take, and just how different are the roles.

Yes?

Of course, there are those who don't believe in such a thing as *The Call*. The debate rages on.

So, let me ask: Why did *you* become a nurse? Are you a healthcare professional whose calling was an empty checkbook? Was there an imperious relative who demanded obedience? Did you search the web for "Best jobs"? Did you close your eyes and pick a profession out of a jar?

Even if you don't have a spiritual calling, the good news is there is likely a place for you in nursing. The bad news is, if caring for another human being at a most vulnerable, i.e., difficult, time of life is NOT your idea of fulfillment, you will have a much better life if you chose a different subject. Nursing is extremely difficult work if you don't love the work.

Having had roles on both sides of the bedrail, and as a nursing instructor, I beg you: If you do not love this work, please find another way to make a living. *Please!*

The opposite is also true (Nightingale agreed), that despite a most difficult, even horrendous day at work, I can always say, "I made a positive difference in at least one person's life today."

We learned how Florence Nightingale's *call* underpinned the integrity that sustained her ability to negotiate change.

What was your launching pad to healthcare? Let me know at candy@candycampbell.com.

# Act I Scene iii

## INTEGRITY IN DISCOVERY: TRAVELS IN EGYPT

I AM HUMBLED TO LEARN that several books have been written about my life. One of them is a fictional work that postulates Mister Gustave Flaubert and I met and knew each other, in biblical terms, in Egypt.[4]

Indeed, we were in Egypt at the same time. I should interject that, had we been in the *very same* place at the same time, I warrant you that my chaperones, the Bracebridges, would never have allowed that social intercourse. No, no, *no!*

That man, however celebrated, was a known rake.

And you must understand, at the time, for myself, as a single woman, to be in another country, even with chaperones, was so highly unlikely. I was, at every turn, protected from the company of strangers, unless said strangers had been previously approved by my chaperones. Mind you, the Bracebridges were duty-bound by friendship and honor, to report any and every bit of our journey worth reporting to my parents, post haste. How else could any responsible parent have given consent for an unmarried daughter to leave the safety of home for several months, to journey to what was known as an uncertain environment? They were very protective in that way.

Now, I would like to say a few words, about my formative trip to Egypt.

(Sigh.)

I wonder how many of you know that this was such a life-altering experience for me?

I had been suffering so, from the time I was nearly seventeen, when I felt that God called me to this new...

Well, I didn't know what He called me to. I was struggling and wrestling, like Jacob. Would the Lord Almighty please, *please* show me the path to my destiny?

One visceral observation kept me awake at night: I could not turn away from the striking and unfortunate societal disparities visible to anyone who chose to look.

It angered me that so few in my acquaintance bothered even to notice those whom Jesus named *the least of these*. It was my dreadful burden, apparently.

My parents expected me to be concerned with trivial pursuits, like all the other gentlewomen. But in my view, they (the gentlewomen) were wasting their lives.

I could not imagine such a life, and it wasn't for want of a suitor, if that's what you were thinking. No, I had more than one suitor for marriage, thank you very much.

Rather, I could not bring myself to be a wife or a mother, because I knew that if I were, it would take me away from what I felt was *my calling*. St. Paul said that 'twas better to be single if one was to accomplish a certain goal, which the Lord has ordained.[5]

I don't believe everyone has to feel the same calling as I did. But I *do* believe that for those of us who have been given a certain *concern*, the Lord will tap one on the shoulder, as it were, and fashion a life choice.

Of course, the will, is our own.

Oh, but let me tell you about traveling to Egypt. My, what an adventure!

Truly, the reason I went was a bit selfish. I was distraught. I had been...

Well, if you have ever spent a winter in the north, you know how bleak weather outside might affect one's inner senses. To me, this combined with my inner struggle and manifested in dolefulness. After all, I was nearly 29 years; an old maid by societal standards. The clock was ticking!

I knew that I was called for something else, but now I'm talking circles. Forgive me.

Ah, the Bracebridges. Selina, my friend (we called her *Sigma*), she was more than a mother to me. She was my angel.

When I was *in a mood* one day, she spoke with me.

I had excused myself from dinner (actually, I ran away from the table), and by all measures, I felt hopeless and confused.

The conversation at table that evening had run its usual tack about my chances for a good marriage fleeting by, and I couldn't abide another word.

While I was weeping in my room, Selina knocked and asked, would I walk with her?

"Your garden is quite lovely this season," she remarked.

As we walked, she said, "My dear, you know Mr. B and I have no children. Now, I'm not quite old enough to be your mother, but I could have been."

She said, "Your parents love you and want the best for you, even though they do not understand about your *call*."

That was an understatement; she had my attention.

"My dear, Mr. B and I have known you a good long time, and we see something special in you. We believe that Providence has called you to some effectual work, whatever that might be. Allow me to be your confidante; I believe in you. With your parent's permission, of course, what might we do to assist you?'"

This conversation couldn't have come at a better time.

I was at a breaking point that day, questioning if *my calling* was pure madness, and I thought I could go no longer without some sort of tangible *sign.* And yet, logic dictates that signs and miracles are mostly unsubstantiated and incorrectly reported. That shows you the depth of my desperation---that I wanted something illogical!

Oh, as you can imagine, to have a friend who believed me was quite enough at the time to encourage and strengthen my faith that God had provided, once again, exactly what I needed.

I laugh now to think I doubted that the Creator of the Universe, who in a word spoke forth all existence, certainly no stranger to miracles, could have given me one small sign. But there it was.

Later, when Selina and Mr. B. asked my parents' permission to take me on an adventure, to *Egypt,* of all places, I could not recall being so enchanted with the mere idea!

Egypt!

So exotic, so primitive, so far from my troubles -- and my parents!

Until we left, I rather drove them mad at home. I would walk, head in the clouds, then sigh and whisper, *Egypt!* I was so keen to discover everything new.

I'm sure my family were as happy to see my coattails, as I was to board the train at Victoria.

The experience of arriving as a tourist in Egypt, you should understand, was totally estranged from the tourism that my family, in our travels to Italy and France, had experienced prior.

As we would say, *on the continent,* at every turn, one sees the art, and all the beauty that has risen forth from centuries of civilized society. It was so lovely on the continent, but *Egypt...*?

This cradle of civilization was...Well, it was nothing but brown! The Nile was brown, the sand was brown, and the people were brown. There was so much to take in, I wrote daily letters home.

There was a sense of desolation in Egypt. There were tombs, catacombs, and dismal people everywhere. Not to mention the flies, and the gnats, the fleas, and the rats. I cannot tell you. The only beauty was in the sky. That deep ebony sky, with an infestation of stars -- more spectacular than I had ever seen.

Well, then it made perfect sense to me, why the Egyptians, as miserable as they might be in this life, had no trouble understanding that there is a life after death. So, the idea of living dismally, as they did, among the ruins, among the sandstorms, the desolation, it made perfect sense. They had reason to be hopeful.

On another note, my friends, I could not believe the cruelty we witnessed. There was a practice called *bastinado,* a punishment, where a poor wretch would be beaten on the soles of his feet. Barbaric! I felt nauseated. This violence was absolutely unjustified. Sometimes the torture was fatal. As tourists, there was nothing any of us could do to stop it. Oh, the misery, the inhumanity we saw, meted out on the *least of these,* in the African countries. It broke my heart.

Of course, when I returned, mother said, "Well, dear, now that you have the wanderlust out of your system, are you ready to marry and settle down?"

And I replied, "No mother. Rather the opposite. 'Tis clear to me, finally, what I must be about!"

I admit, I was taken aback; a touch flummoxed. To receive such a reception, after all the letters that I had written from Egypt, which provided sufficient knowledge to draw from and understand my focused interest in service to humanity? I wrote page, after page, after page, about the cruel conditions there, about man's inhumanity to man, woman, and child, not to mention animals. I was stricken with an urge of hysteria!

How to elude their barefaced questions and suppositions that after all the passion poured out in my epistles home, they should expect me to put down my cross and sit, catlike, in a corner for the rest of my days? Or worse, to give up any hope of my calling, and consent to be shackled to a husband-master like a bird in a cage? I tell you, I was tempted to become a nun, if only to escape. How could I forget the lessons of Egypt? The lessons I was sure Providence provided for good purpose?

But thankfully, my friend *Sigma* understood. She helped convince my family that this new horizon, this nursing profession, was indeed *my calling.* She convinced Father to allow me to take the nurses' training at Kaiserswerth.

However, Egypt was the launching pad.

# PERSPECTIVE ON *DISCOVERY*

I FEEL GREAT AFFINITY with Miss Nightingale for many reasons.

We both spent much time in our formative years pondering universal questions regarding our purpose here on earth, and both of us spent concentrated time traveling and studying other cultures. (I studied in Vienna half a year as an undergrad, then in the course of the next five years, lived in New York, L.A., Sydney, Paris, Cologne, London, and Honolulu.) My work took me to more places than I will take time to list. It was a wonderful education. Read on.

I received *the call* to be a nurse, while working as a flight attendant when 124 passengers vomited -- in unison.

Back-story: One sunny Portland afternoon, when I was a girl, my uncle Gus took my father and me up in his one-engine plane. When he did some loop-de-loops, I screamed, "Whee!" and my dad lost his lunch.

That day, I announced that when I grew up, I was going to be a stewardess.

Fast-forward: A year after I graduated from college with a degree in Speech Communication and Theatre. By that time, I planned to take the acting fellowship I had been offered with the University of Minnesota's prestigious Guthrie

Theatre in their MFA program. I was all set, until life got in the way. Undaunted, I worked on Plan B, which was to go to LA or NYC and carve out an acting career there.

Unfortunately, I experienced a classic *casting couch* encounter with a director that derailed my interest in an acting career. (Call me *picky*, but I also acquired some inconvenient preferences, like wanting more than one meal a day and performing with clothes *on.*)

So, when Pan Am came to town to conduct interviews, I remembered that day in Uncle Gus' plane. I envisioned a way to break free from my parents and see the world. (Sound familiar?)

Back to *my calling*: It was 120 °F on the tarmac in New Delhi when we set out for Karachi, Pakistan. Those were the days when we served a hot meal on nearly every flight. The irony is that early in the flight, I had gone up to the first class cabin to fetch something, and as I passed by, a passenger touched my arm. He was clutching his throat in the classic choking gesture, so I quickly called for help and prepared to do one of my newly learned skills, the Heimlich maneuver. He stopped me. "Not choking; cardiac," he gasped. My crewmates and I administered oxygen, and he stabilized.

When I returned to my station, I told my colleague what happened. She was impressed that I knew what to do and asked if I was a nurse.

"Nope," I said, "My high school counselor told me she doubted if I could pass chemistry. But I think about nursing school every time someone on the plane gets sick."

Later, after having served the heavy lunch, we encountered heavier turbulence. The captain put on the seat belt sign. Just as I got to the jump seat facing the passengers, the plane dropped like a rock. THAT is when my seatmate and I saw the *ribbons of vomit*. It was enough to make her sick, too.

I concluded that when it comes to sickness, some run to help and some run to hide.

When she returned and sat down again, I said, "You know, if it wasn't so sad that people were sick, it was kind of artistic."

"Seriously," she quipped, straight-faced, "you *really* need to consider nursing school."

Did you experience the call? I'd love to include your story in my next book. Write me at candy@candycampbell.com.

# Act II Scene i

## INSIGHT: LESSONS FROM SCUTARI

PEOPLE HAVE ASKED ME, "How ever did you survive the horrors of war?"

Honestly, this question used to bore me. The question told as much about the questioner.

(Usually, this was some well-heeled aristocrat, living in luxury, oblivious to the sufferings of their poorer neighbors in the world at home, as well as on the battlefield. I suppose they imagined me sipping tea from a china cup, while reading the latest society news?)

As a person of faith, you see, that is a non-question. This life is but a journey through a world filled with corruption. For what is war? Is it not when attempts at civil discourse have failed to bridge the chasm of reason and desire, and men are pressed to leave hearth and home and take up arms against their neighbors? Given this assumption, besides the physical discomfort of living out of doors, the soul-sick loneliness and misery that accompanies the spilling of blood, the loss of friends, the fear of death, what else *would* one expect in war? A picnic?

We survived in the same manner that those involved in conflict, ever before, and ever since, must survive: We made a *decision.* We decided to act, come what may.

We decided to do our best with what was provided, to use our senses to find a way around, over, and through adversity. The difficulties we nurses faced, with the leaky roof and windows, that admitted wind, rain, and storm, the lack of decent food, billeted with barely 18 inches between flimsy cots, the filthy surroundings, amounted to *nothing* in comparison to the sacrifices of those brave young men.

Yes, we worked tirelessly, as stand-ins for mothers, sisters, and wives, who could not be present to attend to a son, a brother, a husband. Sometimes, our only reward was to sense that for one brief moment before death, a young man, cut down in the prime of life, felt a touch of kindness, saw a smile, and heard the words, "Thank you for your service. God bless you. Now rest."

During the long journey home, after I shed many tears for the lost lives there, I determined the best route to recovery was to fulfill the promise I made in Scutari. The vision of so many times, as I sat with a soldier who was dying, and played the role of his family member, haunted me. As they called out, in delirium, I answered, "Yes! I will tell him. I will tell her." I wrote the words to send in a letter. I prayed with them, stroked their foreheads, held their hands, heard their confessions, reassured them of the love of God, their family, their country, their comrades, of my admiration for their steadfastness, for a job well done. I told each one, "Now rest, and prepare to enter the joyful place, where there is no pain, no suffering, no tears." And once, at that last moment, as this teenaged boy turned paler still, and I saw his life ebbing away, he opened his watery blue eyes and sighed, "Oh, the singing!"

Each day, I realized anew what a privilege we nurses are afforded, to attend the beginning *as well as* the end of a life. Moreover, my resolution to change the British military system to better provide for those who have given so much for us, was set in stone— *tombstone.*

So, when curious minds ask: What did you take from your time in Scutari? I answer: Besides Brucellosis, I took the impression of those lonely, handsome, young faces---and a determination to effect a change. Indeed, on the long journey home, I felt rather like Alice awakening from her journey through the looking glass: I was ill in body, tormented by remembrances, and bewildered in spirit.

When I arrived home, I opted out of the welcome parade as a grand celebrity. Having endured 22 months of what you might call, *sensory overload,* I could not wait to get home to the lovely quiet of our estate and vegetate for a while. I needed to rest and heal, until I felt strong enough to take on the British military. We owed it to our soldiers.

I remembered my visit to the French Sisters of Charity, there in Scutari. I said, *"Merci beaucoups pour vous me permette visitez votre l'hopital."*

And the French matron replied, "Not at all, it is *notre plaisire.*"

Their hospitals were supplied handsomely and their method of organization was seamless, as the Catholic Church administered it. The difference it made in terms of the services offered, their low infection and mortality rates, not to mention their data collection system, made me confess to envy.

Meanwhile, I had hoped that God would remove the *thorn from my side* once I rested at home. Alas, that was not His plan. I was forced, once again, to make a decision to act, despite my disabilities.

Each day, I would plan my schedule and assess my ability to carry it out. As a nurse, I always had Plan A and Plan B. Often Plan C was put into use. After Turkey, I seldom traveled or left my rooms for more than a brief time. I found this was the most expedient use of my strength. I preferred individual conversations, with one prerequisite: I would see anyone who would be able to put forth my goals. This did not set very well with my family, as I refused to leave London. It was imperative that I would be given access to the news of the day and those who made the news.

And God is good. He proved to me over and over, that one person with faith and a goal, however lofty, and God to sustain it, could move mountains.

# PERSPECTIVE ON INSIGHT
## GAINED FROM WAR

ALTHOUGH I DIDN'T SERVE AS A NURSE IN WAR, I had another experience while working as a flight attendant that became a seed of remembrance. This "seed" grew until I was mature enough to recognize it needed to became a creative tribute to those who gave their lives in an undeclared and unpopular war, not unlike the one in which Miss Nightingale served.

It all started on a trip to Cam Ranh Bay in 1973. Pan Am provided charter service to certain military transport flights during those days. We landed after dark and had an hour layover until the passengers boarded.

Curious, I crept down the stairs to have a look.

I saw two soldiers in dress uniform guarding the bottom of the steps.

I approached, but they refused to speak to me. The Captain said they had orders to be *at attention*. As civilians in a military zone, we were a liability. I took it as a kind of a game, and was joking around, trying to make them laugh, but they were very focused.

Soon my eyes adjusted to the dark of the tarmac, and I watched as the baggage handlers drove the luggage for our passengers around to the cargo hull.

But wait.

As the jeep-led caravan of baggage carts passed closer, the bags looked longer than regular duffel bags.

Suddenly, the realization hit me.

Those weren't duffel bags. Those were *body* bags!

The visceral reaction I felt shocked me. It strikes again, suddenly, as I type these words.

I couldn't face those guards. I turned around. A shiver ran down my arms and suddenly, tears spilled down my chin. This chatterbox was speechless, blubbering at the foot of the stairs.

Feelings of shame and guilt, poured out with those tears, as I remembered a high-school friend who died a hero as he threw himself over a hand grenade to save the lives of his comrades.

At that moment, it felt as though having marched in an anti-war protest parade was an insult to the men who died for me! I know that's illogical. I know that we were really protesting the political mash-up that encouraged such a conflict, but as an American, I felt so useless in the face of war.

I wept for the men cut down in the prime of their lives.

Later in the flight, the men (I agree with Miss Nightingale, they were *boys*) acted upbeat. They were so excited to be able to spend their R&R in Honolulu! Some of them would even be headed home with our flight the next day.

There was only one military woman on that flight. She sat at the back by the galley, and I was working the front of the cabin, so I didn't have a chance to speak with her. One of my colleagues said, "She's' a *nurse.*" I was already thinking about nursing school, so I really wanted to talk to her. Alas, I didn't get the chance.

The next day, I worked the back galley, and surprise -- the Navy nurse, again in her white dress uniform, sat close to the back of the cabin. The flight was only about half full, so I knew I'd have time to approach her.

Finally! The meal was served, the galley cleaned, and I had my chance to speak to my *new best friend.*

I rehearsed the whole conversation. I would say, Hi, I'm Candy, and I'm thinking of going to nursing school. Would you mind if I asked you a few questions?

She would pat the empty seat next to her and invite me to sit down. Then, she would tell me *everything I needed to know and was afraid to ask* about the nursing profession. Yay!

I took a deep breath and approached.

To my shock and dismay, in answer to my question, she kept staring out the window. She barely glanced up. I asked again and she shook her head and waved me away as she sighed, "Noooo."

I was crestfallen. What in the world had happened to her? What had she experienced that created such a reaction to an innocent question?

I was so young and naïve.

When we landed in Oakland International Airport, it looked a lot different than it does today. Passengers disembarked down a long, portable stairway, and walked into the terminal.

One of my duties that day was to stand at the bottom of the staircase, and with my gloved hand, point to the last step and recite the mantra, "Watch your step and thank you or flying Pan Am!"

The Navy nurse was the last passenger off. Our Purser gave the go-ahead sign, and I followed about twenty paces behind the Navy nurse, into the terminal.

It was a beautiful spring day, and I can recall watching the light as it streamed through the transom windows. Lovely.

Then I heard something that turned my stomach. There were several *hippie*-types standing on the left, by the rail that separated us. They were yelling malicious epithets to the men in front, and now the Navy nurse.

One called her a *baby-killer*. Another one hocked a loogie and spat right at her cheek!

I will always remember the way the Navy nurse never even broke stride. She continued forward, and with one smooth circle gesture, took out her handkerchief, wiped her cheek, and returned it to her pocket.

As I passed the hecklers, I wanted to yell back, "Stop it!" but I didn't.

There was no one brave there but the veterans.

I caught up with her at one of the three baggage carousels, as we waited for our bags.

"I'm so sorry! Those people are awful!"

"Never mind," she said, deadpan. "If that's the worst that happens today..." and she trailed off in thought.

Oh, my goodness. My *new best friend* has worked in conditions this little spoiled brat from the 'burbs can't even imagine.

I hid that scene in my heart for nearly 30 years before I learned enough to write about it. I spent a year interviewing nurses and others who had served in Vietnam, then made her the heroine of my fiction, as a tribute.

I hope she sought help for the PTSD she obviously carried home with her as her *souvenir* of the war, and that she lived a good long life after. She might still be alive today. I also pray I have done her justice in my characterization.[6]

As a nurse, what events have helped mature you and give you direction?

What challenges presently help give you insight into your day, your week, and your life?

Please write candy@candycampbell.com and tell me. I'd like to feature your story in my blog.

# Act II Scene ii

## INSIGHTS ON PROGRESS, MISSION, SPEAKING UP

(MISS NIGHTINGALE IS SEEN, head bowed, in silent prayer. She looks up.)

When in Scutari, I was thankful for the call to prayer from the minarets, so that five times a day, my prayerful thoughts were added to theirs, for *all* humankind. There lies a powerful lesson.

Now, as I observe your *modern* society...Oh, that is an amusing adjective each successive era substitutes as its own!

In your modern society, I note the universal questions are still being asked through art: (sings) *Are we human, or are we dancers?* I think we're both. Call me old fashioned, but that certainly has more appeal than urinating on religious icons. (Points for novelty, perhaps? Or animism?)

The subject at hand is progress. How should we define *progress*?

41

Now, let me make something perfectly clear. In my life, the only woman who would have publicly addressed an audience, like this august body, was Her Majesty, the Queen. And so, *my* voice progressed through the *printed word*: 200 books and white papers, and over 15,000 of my letters have been published so far. (One afternoon at tea, my sister said I had diarrhea of the mouth. Mother nearly fell out of her chair!)

Of course, I had no distractions. No radio, no telephone, certainly no television, or Internet. The only mobile device I ever owned was a cane.

Well, times have changed. Although I once lacked self-confidence in front of crowds, or cameras, or strangers, my time on *the other side* has infused me with such joy, I feel willing and able to share with you today, even in the "spoken word poetry" way.

Like yours, my story is difficult to relegate to one category. It is simultaneously an adventure, a comedy, a tragedy, throw in a bit of romance (not much), and a story of redemption. The theme varied, depending upon the decade, the time of day, and the degree of pain or debilitation experienced, thanks to my chronic *souvenir* of the Crimean War. (I have mentioned it: Brucellosis. Today, it would be easily cured with proper antibiotic therapy. Along with the sciatica, this was my thorn in the side, so to speak.)

Shakespeare said, "All the world's a stage, and we, merely players. We have our entrances and our exits..." [7] The constant here, like a stream running through it, were my family, friends, and the colleagues who crossed my path, my cast of characters. They helped challenge me, and so I grew and progressed.

Who challenges you? You notice I did not say, who flatters you and tells you what of your lovely personage ? To whom do you look for honesty in any situation? Such friendship, such mentoring is better by far than riches. But I digress.

Ah, yes, *progress.*

In my life, I experienced change: from horses, to iron horses, to horseless carriages. You have gone from planes, to rockets, to space stations. I listened to Schubert, Brahms, and Strauss. You hear The Beatles, Green Day, and EDM.

In my life, I saw windmills and candles replaced by steam and gas. You have gone from electricity, to solar, and back to windmills.

My generation saw many deadly eruptions, from the Crimean Conflict, to your Civil War, to Krakatoa, Mt. Pelee, and the Russian Revolution.

Since then, you have seen too many to count. From Sarajevo to Hitler, to Korea, Hiroshima, Vietnam, Tiananmen Square, Mt. St. Helens, Chernobyl, to 9-11, the oil spills, to Iraq, Rwanda, suicide bombings, to Afghanistan, Oklahoma City, Columbine and Newtown, to group beheadings...and back to the Crimean conflict.

You call this *progress?*

Everyone. Take a deep breath. *(She breathes deeply.)*

That's better.

Indulge me while I make the application.

One mystery that we love to watch unfold down here, is what has been partially revealed about the cosmos.

No doubt you, astute audience that you are, have knowledge of the existence of the *death star?*

(Oh, another rhyme slipped out. I seem to have lost control. It's like passing gas.)

Fascinating! And about death stars, as well.

Since you do not yet have my perch (*she looks up*), let me tell you: A death star is an accumulation of gases in an elementary form. That is: sulfur, magnesium, silicon, and finally, iron. These elements roll around in space, the hands of gravity pressing in upon each other, rather like a giant kneading dough, 'til the heaviest element, iron, sinks to the center. In so doing, it ssssucks in the rest of the star, until it CONSUMES itself, from the inside out. Then, it collapses...into *nothingness.*

If you study this phenomenon, you'll find it is this heavy weight at the star's core that predicts its death.

Now here's the application: A parallel illustration is the element of *pride,* in far too many healthcare organizations, which *weighs heavily at the top, like the iron at the center of a star.* An inflated sense of self-worth in the leadership team is the iron that fuels its ultimate collapse.

Now, ladies and gentlemen of this esteemed convocation, I have come here today with a message to facilitate the beginning of your personal and organizational *progress.*

Of course, you realize that the prequel to any change must be facilitated. Whether by an attitude of curiosity, a need to solve a problem, or a mistrust of the status quo, a mind-set of adaptation must prevail. Some might call it a healing of sorts, as forgiveness is often a necessary element before a change can be effected.

My message is ever the same, despite the circumstances, and it hinges upon your knowledge that you are a child of the Omnipotent, and that you have a mission in life to fulfill. You may already know it.

Perhaps, though, the mission is so great, and the apprehension of duty so overwhelming, you have abandoned it. But I am here to persuade you to recall that it takes a very small rudder to turn around the largest sailing vessel. Indeed, one person *can* and has always been able to make a difference. (Whether the difference be for evil or good, this universal truth is undeniable.)

Now, now, I see some of you are beginning to squirm. Please, before you tune me out, hear me out. Your *mission challenge* requires an attitude of gratitude, as He who humbled himself and died for us all. Think of someone whose leadership you admire. For me, faith and the attitude of gratitude was the basis of all practical activity here on earth.

Happily, according to the latest scientific research, faith and an attitude of gratitude will sustain you mentally and physically, as well. As scientists, when we study the world, we cooperate with The Universal to discover His laws, and then intervene for good. Simply put, faithful, grateful, humble people live longer, experience more health, and more joy than anyone else.

Enough said. This is not a sermon, but it is only meet, right, and salutary, that you should understand the underpinnings of everything I did in my life, both personal and professional, hinged upon a spiritual center.

Oh, yes, let me add, that when I heard about your Big Bang Theory, I didn't bat an eye. The laws of entropy notwithstanding, logic dictates that if the Lord spoke the world into existence, it made quite a ruckus. Creation of anything is a messy business.

Furthermore, it should not surprise modern minds to discover that science is intensely intricate, and immensely original, as is the work of any artist. My contention always was this: We were placed here to be the loving stewards of this amazing planet *and* of each other.

# PERSPECTIVE ON IRON AT THE TOP AND SPEAKING UP

AS I THINK ABOUT THESE QUESTIONS, I recall certain events in my life that propelled me to find the courage to speak up. Each one led me closer to nursing and public health advocacy. Here's the story of one of them:

While in nursing school, I worked part time as a Burn Unit Tech. One day we were short-staffed, and the Charge Nurse asked me to take vital signs and sit with a newly received post-surgical patient, while she finished up with another patient. She said she would be right back.

The patient was about my same age, worked as a psychiatric tech, and had been lit on fire by a patient.

She had several intravenous lines, an indwelling urinary catheter, a tracheostomy, and was bandaged head to toe.

Evidently, a deranged psych patient had thrown lighter fluid in her face and upper torso, and then struck a match. As a result, she had multiple skin grafts taken from her lower body. She looked like mummy; the only skin I could see was on her fingers and toes.

I still had a year to go to finish nursing school and had never been that close to a ventilator or a trach. Suddenly water started to form in the vent tubes and tripped the alarm. Then the IVs started alarming. I called for assistance, as the patient regained consciousness and started to moan. She obviously needed pain medication, too.

Now, anyone who knows what a process it is to maintain *reverse isolation* for the sake of immunocompromised patients understands that to get in and out of a burn patient room is not a quick process.

It was necessary to de-glove, de-gown, remove mask and booties, and wash my hands, just in order to exit to the non-sterile area of the room where the phone was hanging on the wall.

Needless to say, I was not prepared to care for this patient, and I was scared spitless. Furthermore, I was not licensed to care for this patient. My job description was to assist the RN, not to replace an RN.

I reached for the phone, reported my findings, and called for help.

Unfortunately, this occurred *back in the day* before Rapid Response Teams were created. Help was *not* on the way. In fact, when I pleaded with the Charge Nurse to please hurry and give the patient some pain med, she told me she was too busy, and that I should just give it myself. She drew up the medication in a syringe and handed it to me.

I couldn't believe it.

There was no justification or legal right for me to give that medication without supervision (especially a medication I didn't personally prepare). If I gave it, I could see my chance for licensure flying out the window. Even if I had given it, the patient still would need an RN stat.

I began to shake with the moral distress of knowing that my poor patient was suffering, but that to help her might cost me my career.

I said to the Charge Nurse, "Please, don't ask me to do that. You know I'm not licensed. The patient needs an RN. I've called the respiratory therapist for the ventilator beeps, but I don't know how to handle all these lines."

By this time, all the alarms were going off, the patient was moaning loudly, and the dressings on her head had become completely saturated with blood. The urinary bag had filled to the top in the last half hour, her blood pressure was falling, and her heart rate was increasing. She was clearly going into shock!

She needed help fast. I grabbed the phone and called the operator to page the in-house supervisor *stat.*

When relief arrived, it was the end of the shift. I was told to go home and *not say anything to anyone.*

The next day, I learned that the Charge Nurse had filed a report of misconduct, stating that I was incompetent to work in critical care!

Interesting: The management said I would be *allowed* to keep my job and transfer to a different department, *if* I promised to keep quiet.

Immediately, I sought the advice of an attorney, who counseled that it would take a lot of time, money, and grief to sue the hospital, and the stress of it all might negatively impact my studies. He was right, of course, and I knew it. This was a David and Goliath situation, and I was the wimp without a slingshot. I kept my mouth shut.

Although I do not know whatever happened to the Charge Nurse who made a false report about me, I have chosen to forgive her, and pray that she sought counseling. Dishonesty among healthcare professionals is a frightening and dangerous concept, all around. The corporate liability goes without saying, for refusing to keep *on call* nurses in that critical care unit.

However, there is a bright side to this dark story.

Because of that incident, I became an active member of our local chapter of the National Student Nurses Association, with a special interest in educating and equipping student nurses about their legal rights and responsibilities.

I learned about public health policy, served on the State Board of Directors as the Editor of the newspaper, and began to speak at conferences. I continue to advocate for nurses and the public in health policy, with the American Nurses' Association, and Sigma Theta Tau, Nursing Honor Society.

What gives you joy? What causes you to wither or speak up? How do you define your mission? And what is progress? How do you advocate for your profession?

I'm interested to know your answers to all of these questions, so we can share in future webinars. Write me at candy@candycampbell.com.

# Act Ⅱ Scene ⅲ

## INSIGHTS TO THE
## FEMINIST MYSTIQUE

SPEAKING OF PROGRESS, one of the myths I must take this time to deflect revolves around the issue of self-confidence, as opposed to pride and / or humility. I see them on a continuum. Pride at one end, humility on the other, and self- confidence somewhere towards the humility side of the middle.

People often assume that because I did manage to launch out onto an entirely different path, I possessed an unusual capacity of self-determination and confidence. I am here to attest to the disingenuous nature of that supposition. Specifically, I never considered myself an ally with the feminist camp, except in general terms. I believed I was a *modern*, and that logic taught that if all people were created equally, then all women should be allowed to find some good work, and to do it.

If you knew me, you would know I was by nature a contended and compliant young person, not given to rebelliousness. As an adult, I still preferred action to speech making and demonstrations. Perhaps that is why, when I finally broke loose at the age of 31 and took the position as Superintendent at the *Institution for Sick Gentlewomen in Distressed Circumstances,* I launched into the work with passion. It felt so good to be useful!

My goal was to pursue excellence in all duties and responsibilities accorded me, however few.

Father tutored me in Greek, Latin, German, French, and Italian. I sought to be an eager student so that I could read the classics, from Euripides, to Socrates, and Plato. I discovered such joy through Euclid and mathematics, then statistics. It makes me giddy to think of it! I wished that all young women had had an opportunity to learn as I did. (Alas, it would be many years before women could be admitted as university scholars.)

Besides the joy of study, there was no other way to attain my goal but through the means afforded me, that is, my father's good graces.

My eventual triumph to leave parental protection and take a few months of nurses' training in Germany was more like unto the persistent dripping of a faucet, according to my father, than any threatening behavior.

Later, my tenure in that hellhole, Scutari, afforded me what I believe you would now refer to as *street credentials*. That experience would change my life in so many ways.

After my return, as a professional nurse, and statistician, and because of my social standing, I was able to address the problems of disorganization and incompetence within the military hospital system, and by extension, to organize my civilian hospital nursing education plan. This was exhausting work, and it did not follow easily, nor did it end particularly well for the military reorganization plan.

However, my next project, the school of nursing, exists today. The ideas for both were conceived as we watched young men die there in Scutari.

It was many years and many projects completed before I ceased to anguish with self-doubt. Understand, I had no doubts that God had called me to service, but I languished daily over decisions I had reached and whether I could have done better. I suspect there are many of you with these same feelings?

It is indeed lonely in any leadership position.

As an aside, I might add that another benefit of the transformation from this life to the next is that instantly all mysteries were revealed to me. While I am not at liberty to disclose any that have not yet been uncovered, I may say how pleased I was to learn about the latest research on happiness.

Not surprisingly, one of the requirements of a satisfied life is that we surround ourselves with people we care about and who care about us. It's the we/us instead of the I/me frame of mind, which brings about the greatest peace and joy in this life, despite one's economic circumstances.

While we are never able to choose our family of origin, nor our in-laws, we are always able to choose our friends. Again I say, an attitude of gratitude leads you to find friends, when you seek them out.

You may find that in spite of great opposition of character, you became steady friends with someone you never chose to enter your path. This happened many times in my life, as I sought to put forth a public health agenda.

And so, my recommendation is that all of you use your experience and your worst nightmares to light a fire in your soul, to reshape healthcare policy. I beg you, do not stand by and assume that your one, small voice can do nothing to change the status quo.

Of course, I understand, not every nurse will be able to be a spokesperson. I know it all too well. I toiled the better part of my last fifty years in attempt to un-gag nurses and encourage them to speak up! Truly, that was no fault of their own.

The times have changed, but sometimes, I think, not so much. The ingrained social hierarchy manages to maintain inertia.

We must go and sit at the table -- lest we find ourselves on the menu.

# PERSPECTIVE ON THE
# FEMINIST MYSTIQUE

I ALSO ADMIRE AND HOPE TO REPLICATE Miss Nightingale in the methods she chose to advance her causes. How? Whenever she aligned herself to a cause, people knew, as a scholar, that she had taken the time to study both sides of the argument. As a woman of principle and means, people believed that her opinions carried no motives for personal gain.

She also knew the toll she would pay as a contrarian. It's lonely there at the front of the line. Roger's diffusions of innovations theory says that *innovators* begin a paradigm shift with ideas that are not shared by the herd. Eventually, the paradigm shifts, but it takes time.

Speaking of time, we baby boomers reached adulthood on the cusp of a cultural change. Amazing, isn't it, that women still earn less than men for the same work?

Regrettably, the occasions in my life when I stood up for my rights as a woman have been few. The first I can recall was after I announced to my family that I would like to go to college. My father had expected my brothers to go and had paid their way. To me, he said, "Why don't I just burn the money?" I won out with scholarships that mostly paid my way, and I can still hear him tell people, "Yep. She's goin' to college. She's playing hard and studying theater!" And then he would laugh. My parents made sure I had an education minor so I could get an education *and* a job.

I faced another feminine crisis a few years later, when I was raped. I regret that I didn't speak up about it. I was ashamed to have been so trusting of someone I thought I knew. I blamed myself for the situation, since I had agreed to go into to this person's apartment, so he could "change clothes." I was so naïve. Afterwards, I felt stupid and used. (Note: I didn't even hear the term *date rape* until many years later.) Now, I look back and thank heavens it was in the days before HIV/AIDs.

Still, it wasn't until I was a nurse that I grasped the concept that we must be caretakers of our one resource: our bodies. Also, that we are all one breath away from eternity. Most of us chose to forget that.

What insights have you learned from reading about Miss Nightingale? Let me know at candy@candycampbell.com.

# Act III Scene i

## INNOVATION: LOCAL CHANGES

I WAS ASKED TO COMMENT of the role of innovation on my work.

Mother always said I plagued her with "too many questions." So, no doubt, innovation is foreshadowed by a curious mind. Also, I spent many an hour in imaginative play, which mimicked the sorts of problems to which my sister and I were exposed, being raised on a large estate with the work of daily living going on all about us. Father said our homes, and surrounding villages were a microcosm of the universe.

I think the key is to be open to outside ideas and have an overarching goal that is more important than oneself. I dreamt of a society where healthcare is a right, not a privilege. There were so many public health inequities then, not only within the military.

However, in order to push the dream forward, we needed nurses who were educated differently. At the time, there was no nursing education template in England. I recalled what I had seen in the French hospitals and what I had begun in Scutari and imagined the best case-scenario. In this way, I fashioned the nurse's curriculum and presented the idea to the Army officials at the Ministry of War. My undeserved notoriety served as a propellant to launch what became the Nightingale School of Nursing at St. Thomas' Hospital, the oldest school of nursing in the UK.

I determined my next project would be to ease the sufferings of the poor women and children born to them in the workhouses in Britain. In time, that became a reality, as well.

My grandest dream was of a national healthcare system for the poor, as the rich had means to seek all the care they needed. Alas, I did not live to see it.

Meanwhile, my associations with civil engineers while in Turkey allowed me to link to projects that I never could have dreamed. Their innovations inspired me!

India, you see, was brewing about then. The troubles there posed some intriguing problems in terms of public health, as well as their system of governance. I met with five consecutive Viceroys to India between 1863 and 1888, plus many other officials in London. We planned the first of several public health and environmental reform projects, in the study at my rooms.

After India, I counseled representatives from the United States, Canada, Australia, Switzerland, and New Zealand. We collaborated to devise similar systems to help prevent disease and eradicate cholera, just as we had done in Scutari.

So, innovation requires curiosity as one trait, but it must be accompanied by a great deal of imagination and hard work. That clever Mr. Einstein said, "Imagination is more important than knowledge."[8] I quite agree. I would add 'tis better to die ten times in the surf, heralding the way to a new world, than to stand idly on the shore, and be swept away by the oncoming tide.[9]

# PERSPECTIVE ON INNOVATION: UNUSUAL PERSPECTIVE

NURSES THE WORLD OVER have assimilated Miss Nightingale's practice of innovation. An example that stands out in my mind is the group of US Navy nurses stationed in the Philippines and captured in WWII. Although they suffered along with the men, as they were marched as POWs to Bataan[10], they continued to practice the profession of caring with few supplies: eyes to see the hurt, ears to listen to the pain, hands to steady one another, lips to verbalize kindness and keep hope alive. Nurses, you hold these supplies in your caring hearts.

Within the world of the NICU, I am acquainted with several nurses who have helped shape clinical practice with their innovations. One colleague developed a silicone gel pad to use as a cushion to support the delicate heads of our preemie population. Another used 2x6 gauze pads and fashioned the prototype that eventually became micropreemie diapers. No doubt you have examples of your own.

As healthcare professionals, we may offer many innovations to our practice. Sometimes this sounds like complaining, but I prefer to reflect on these sessions as necessary and transitional. How else will we develop the newest ideas? The difference may be the change in thinking from, "Yes, but..." to "Yes, and..."

I recall one such "Yes, and..." innovation that occurred in a med-surg unit during my nursing school days at the VA hospital in Los Angeles. We visited twice weekly and were given this directive: Assist the nursing staff to solve our assigned patient problem.

My patient was a jovial gentleman in his mid-60's who always wore a US Marines cap that covered his balding pate. His wife of forty plus years was often at his side. They were a great team, as they joked with each other and the staff.

Still, his problem was perplexing.

He verbalized frustration that the system of healthcare professionals had been unable to eradicate what seemed like a simple rash on the anterior aspect of his scrotum. So far, he had received two different antibiotics, and various types of creams to heal the sore that had appeared in the center of the rash and looked like a syphilis chancre.

My first day on the case, we received lab results that determined the sore was not syphillic. That news was a relief to everyone and spawned another stream of jokes between the couple.

The technical problem was that this patient, to put it discretely, was *well endowed*, and his *unit* rested on his *package*, so to speak.

My challenge was to find a way to aerate the area.

Nurses had suggested he keep his *unit* diverted to the side. He informed them that his *unit* had a mind of its own, and unless he were to spend the day holding it in the diverted position, it would quickly find it's way back to what he called *ready position.*

As nursing students, this exercise of the nursing process was to spend our first day gathering facts, in order to make a plan. The next day, we were to arrive with the written plan, explain it to our instructor and the patient, and have it approved by the nursing management.

After counseling with the patient that day, I went home and asked expert advice from my husband, as well.

The next clinic day, after submitting our written explanations, my instructor told us all to gather any needed supplies, explain the procedure to the patient, obtain the patient's approval, proceed with the process, and call her to inspect our work, prior the arrival of nursing management.

By the time I had finished patient vital signs, assessment, linen change, and patient personal care, it was lunchtime.

I gathered supplies and found the patient enjoying his meal. That day was a holiday of some sort, so a mini American flag, attached to a toothpick, sat atop the cupcake. Ever the patriot, he made quite a ceremony of removing the flag and placing it in the brim of his hat.

"It needs to fly high," he explained.

Meanwhile, I pushed an IV pole close to the bed, about midway between his head and feet, and pulled the privacy curtain.

I unraveled the thin roll of stretchy gauze, and with the wife's assistance, attached the gauze to the midportion of the patient's *unit*. Then, we fastened the gauze carefully to the IV pole, effectively solving the aeration problem.

Try as we might to be serious, this was a process that caused all three of us to giggle; as the husband quipped he hadn't had this kind of attention since before they were married and he was stationed overseas! (Imagine the patient in the other bed, listening to this?)

Process in place, I went to search for my instructor. When she pulled back the curtain, we saw the patient and his wife, grinning ear to ear, with the little American flag tucked into the gauze!

That process was deemed a safety hazard by management but overruled by the patient. He explained that after only four hours, my unconventional idea caused such an improvement in the problem, he and his wife planned to jury-rig something like it after discharge.

Like me, you may find some of your innovations are more successful than others. Or perhaps you have been too stifled to even attempt a "Yes, and..." change? I challenge you now, don't take my word for it, but try it! I guarantee that the "Yes, and..." mindset will change your professional practice and as well as your personal life.

Please write to me at candy@candycampbell.com so that I may learn from you and pass your innovative ideas on to others!

# Addendum

## Q&A

THESE ARE QUESTIONS COMMONLY ASKED in the interactive portion of the *Channeling Florence Nightingale* presentation. You may find many of them in video form at the *Go With the Flo* blog.

**Q:** What is your insight about nursing in the 21st Century?

**A:** Nurses and other health care professionals now have the benefit of much advanced science with pharmaceuticals and medical devices. I perceive, however, there persist many problems.

It seems ironic to need to enunciate the principle that the overarching goal of a hospital would be to do the patient no harm.[11] Considering the improvements of your century, it shocks me in that regard. There are, obviously, many opportunities for improvement.

Hospitals were never meant to take in the whole of the sick population.[9] My assertion all along has been that hospitals are to be an intermediate stage of civilization. That opinion has not changed. I'm told your "modern" hospitals now harbor a host of *super microbes* (most unfriendly) to all concerned.

I maintain that ultimately, in most cases, 'tis more pleasurable for the patient and family, more cost effective, and reaps better results, if a patient is treated at home.

Naturally, this is not always possible. In the case of surgery or technical care needed to keep a patient alive, but that accounts for a small percentage of the total population.

This reminds me of the premise of my writings about the difference between "sick nursing and health nursing." [12] Nowadays, the same premise has been renamed -- I believe you call it *holistic care.* When I first heard that term, I thought, "That's a bit of alright...has a nice ring to it."

Yes, holistic care...I called it "health nursing," which is taking care of the whole person, not merely the disease or ailment. This involves including the family, providing a calm and clean environment, palatable food, good water.

And that reminds me how surprised I was to learn of your World Health Organization's 'Millennium Development Goals!'

Oh, make no mistake, they are excellent goals: Clean water, improved sanitation, children's nutritional health, health education all around...Who could argue with such demands? Indeed, I began this discussion over 100 years ago.

The question is, "Where's the progress?" Sadly, the confounding variable is the same in your generation as mine: politics and politicking. I say, let's stop talking and get busy doing what needs to be done. I can hear you protest, "How?"

You begin with one small change. You know the one -- the one that keeps you up at night. Tackle that and the next problem will follow. (They always do.)

I know you can succeed! Because you are a nurse—you are resourceful!

**Q:** What is your opinion of the HIV/AIDS virus?
**A:** To discuss the HIV/AIDS virus, I must digress a bit.

In my time, we also had various public-health scourges. It seemed odd to me that so many faithful were praying to be delivered from these plagues, pestilence, and famine. When all the while, the public sewers emptied straightaway into the Thames River, which provided not only public transportation, but drinking and bathing water as well.

As a result, the un-drained ground on the banks of the Thames was haunted with fever. It was a predictable situation with a solemn outcome. As anyone with half a wit and one eye could see. Oh, I could tell you stories about the politicking that went on about that!

But to the point: I believed the cholera came so that we might remove the causes, not to pray that God would remove the cholera! [13]

Now, back to *your* question. We might make the same assertion for any of your modern diseases. Indeed, I devoted quite a lot of thought to this subject. You might like to read more about it in my book with the clever title: *Suggestions for Thought for Searchers after Religious Truth*. It's three volumes.

**Q:** What do you think about the Affordable Healthcare Act in America?
**A:** Certainly, I am generally in favor of any public health policy that is concerned with the poor. In this case, 'tis difficult to form an opinion when the horse is still in the barn, so to speak, and one can only see its nose.

I'll say this about that: good intentions are never enough. Organizational blunders have a ripple effect and can do as much harm as some direct assaults. Compared to premeditated lawlessness, organized carelessness is more hurtful,[14] as you have seen at the rocky beginning of the plan.

I have no objection and would be quite enthusiastic, to be sure, over a healthcare system that would benefit patients, help prevent chronic disease, keep families intact, and overall increase public health. That would be beneficial. Indeed, I advocated my whole adult life for such improvements.

So, when you ask me what is my opinion, I prefer to speak in risk ratios. However, at this writing, retrospective data is not available to make such predictions. I'm reminded that even a keen racing enthusiast would hesitate to wager on a new pony they hadn't seen run. Ah, yes, politics often resembles a racetrack. What a pity people's lives are at stake. 'Tis a gamble, but I am hopeful.

Whether this is the vehicle to complete the task? You shall have to wait and see.

**Q:** If you could go back to school today, what would you study?
**A:** Ah, I am pleased you surmise that I would continue to be a student! Indeed, you have assumed correctly.

To the point, immediately I think of two subjects that interest me: One is computer science and programming. The coding process is key to much innovation. The other is improvisation, whether in music, theatre, or dance. As an educational process, I'm captivated by it. I'm told the applied theatrical exercises are a marvelous tool to encourage interprofessional harmony and open one's mind to innovation.

Again, these are implements with which to navigate the realms of problem solving and to discover new capabilities. There is still much to be learned in your century.

**Q:** What advice would you give to nurses in leadership positions?
**A:** First, be generous with praise and cautious with criticism. You know, nurses and other healthcare professionals do not, generally, set out to harm anyone. With rare exceptions, clinicians only seek to be helpful. Generally, we punish ourselves more than any discipline one could meet out.

Of course, this is not always the case. People do occasionally join our ranks for self-aggrandizement, but they are the exception, not the rule. And for that reason, as leaders, we must approach a non-lethal mistake as an opportunity for improvement, both personally and systemically.

Second, a leader must have control of ones' emotions, and exercise leadership without appearing to exercise it. To have a mind given to impartiality is quite important. And I would add, to prayerfully seek wisdom and guidance at all turns should add a spirit of humility to our work. After all, as the nurse leader must spend less time at the bedside, he or she should consider their work now to include a twofold client base: the patient, whom the nurses serve, and the nurses themselves.

And here's another point I must emphasize: leaders must know when to quit an idea, a policy, what have you, and move on. There is no sense whatsoever in working hard at what does not work! To continue to do the same thing over and over and expect different results would be the definition of madness!

To change your workflow, indeed anything in life, you must open up to new possibilities and change your mind! How can you accomplish this if you shut yourself up in an office and have no contact with anyone who might disagree with you? Seek out those dissenters. Sit down with them. Listen to their concerns. Enlist their help to find workable alternatives! When you lead in this way, you will earn the respect of others, who likely view anyone above them in the hierarchy as a foe.

I love the saying that *feedback is the breakfast of champions!* Whenever possible, I walked the wards with a notepad and pencil and two hands ready to assist. You know, the power to change resides within you alone.

**Q:** What is your definition of a "good nurse"?
**A:** Those who describe a "good nurse" as "devoted and obedient" are guilty of slander. That definition would do just as well for a porter--or for a horse![15]

Nurses are more like policemen, keeping watch over the public health, sounding the alarm and involving the detectives when necessary. Now, you wouldn't want to define a policeman as merely devoted and obedient would you?

Our watchword, like any first responder, should amount to this: Be prepared!

And how do we do that? By constantly expanding our knowledge base. To be sure, knowledge is power.

Those nurses who are content to put in their hours, and never make time to read the latest research? The thought makes me downcast. (Oh, you blessed group, what I would have given to have such a plethora of research to consider!)

**Q:** Were you a Christian Mystic?
**A:** I'm quite sure I never labeled myself anything other than a professional nurse, a statistician, and a Christian, in no particular order.

If I had to venture an opinion, I suppose, a product of a pluralistic society, might want to believe I fancied myself a *mystic.*

For what is mysticism, if tis not the attempt to draw near to God? Not by rites, or ceremonies, but by inward disposition. Is it not merely a synonym for "the kingdom of heaven is within?" [16] Well, if that makes me a mystic, then so be it.

But I assure you, I never owned, nor ever kept, a crystal ball, an Ouija board, a book of spells, or anything of the sort. I could have made use of a flying carpet, but I never found one...

**Q:** What do you have to say about the problem of "bullying"?
**A:** Regretfully, this problem is as old as the nursing profession. Like any complex problem, this topic deserves a view from many angles.

In a systems analysis, such behavior might be considered a nuisance that causes unrest and calamity in the workplace, but let us not paint the problem with too small a brush. This is not only a systems problem, but a developmental one as well.

Allow me to define the terms with a basic understanding of the human condition.

We are all, at the core, spiritual beings. Surrounded, as it were, by layers of the soul, and further encapsulated by the body. We're rather like a hard-boiled egg: body, soul, and spirit. We understand the body and spirit, but what is this thing we call the *soul*?

We shall define the soul as tripartite: the mind or intellect, the emotions, and the will. These three work together to guide our choices. Make sense?

Given that definition, I believe, incivility is essentially a soulful problem; because at the core, our worldview underpins our thoughts, words, and deeds.

The question is: Whom do you serve? If we put ourselves first, we measure moral standards by our own vagaries. Hence, when we find ourselves in a society of self-centered individuals, the results are narcissistic and predictable. It always leads to chaos.

With nurses, we profess to be not only compassionate, in the emotional sense, but caring, which by my definition, is choosing to launch concern into action. But when people are drawn into a profession more by what they can receive than by what they are prepared to give... The opposite is also true.

I think that is the prescient mechanism you describe. This self-centeredness is an age-old problem. The Bible calls it: sin.

We may desire to contain it, nip it in the bud, or squelch this incivility with education, new policies, or re-programming, but those activities will yield no fruit...unless we address the central problem, the heart.

The DNA of a modern nurse is the interface of technology, innovation, cooperation, and hope. In order for progress to be made, the individual's *raison d'etre* in nursing needs be altruistic.

The first thing we must do, when faced with any evil, and I do not hesitate to call this kind of behavior evil, is:

1. Dialogue with the other party. Learn about their underlying pain that causes them to harass someone else. (And you do have an obligation to learn if there is improper function or professional behavior on the part of the bullied as well.)

2. Aid the victims any way you are able.

3. Defend the stance against bullying by taking action: you cannot legislate morality, but you should stand firm on the beliefs of professionalism that include caring---for colleagues as well as patients. Put forth time and effort to tear down walls and build bridges. There are helpful techniques to accomplish this.

I see the problem as based on immaturity. I'm speaking here of soulful immaturity, of course. If you find yourself an object of slanderous talk, first, consider the source. The person or persons may be jealous for some reason, or suspicious of any change you propose, because some people find solace in familiarity and are merely adverse to forward thinking of any kind. I'm quite familiar with this kind of opposition.

If you ask my advice, I'd say ignore them as you would an impertinent child. Do not stoop to their level. Continue functioning as a team player, with the best in mind for those you serve, that is, the patient.

The Golden Rule should be liberally employed in every aspect of our lives. By so doing, you will, as the scriptures say, "heap hot coals of kindness"[17]on their heads.

Against kindness, there is no law. Indeed, it should be your weapon of choice at all times. Then, if, despite your efforts, you find the situation unbearable, my advice is to pray and seek wisdom and guidance as to whether this is indeed a door closing for you.

Meanwhile, what if you look deep within your soul and realize it is you who has been the occasional bully? I admit I have confessed it myself, at times.

How many of us have never let a complaint of a colleague pass our lips?

Think about the times when we find ourselves working long hours with the inevitable workflow problems that occur, when we are tired and hypoglycemic, how many of us have NOT spoken a bit curtly to a colleague? Hopefully, we find the grace to ask forgiveness later.

A new nurse, especially, may wilt at our frustration with whatever it is that they don't seem to understand. This infraction or lack of plan might be to us, the more experienced nurse, so elementary. We forget, my friends, what it is to be a novice.

It is interesting, I think, when speaking of human behavior, that when we suffer a perceived injury, we want justice from the perpetrator. However, when we fall short, we expect mercy.

Trust me on this: Upon your deathbed, this dilemma will seem insignificant -- a tempest in a teapot. For now, trust God, be kind, and make no excuses.

**Q:** Did you experience "burnout"?
**A:** Compassion fatigue and moral distress, commonly called *burnout* was common in my time as well. I believe families understood that adequate nutrition, proper sleep, and supportive family and friends were key to

regaining a sense of balance. I daresay, this is the essence of the problem.

In nursing, when we are short staffed or asked to work incredibly long hours, there will be fallout. We named it soul sick, bilge, noxious by-products, or plain *tiredness*.

Faced with the burden of the reality of sickness and death, my only answer was and is faith; faith, that this world, however full of pain, suffering, and evil, also holds joy, peace, and goodness.

And like soldiers, when we step away from the battle we fight with sickness and death, we are able to rest if we can put our trust in One who sees all and knows all, and who will someday, somehow, work it all out to the best good. (I'm happy to report the truth of this statement, but I am unable to elaborate.)

I do not purport to have understood these mysteries while I was a sojourner here on earth, and I am quite aware that we cannot win every battle.

If I might speak frankly, when I was bound to this mortal coil, like you, I wrestled much with the problem of man's inhumanity to man. My conclusion is that wars is hell, and make no mistake, all in the healthcare professions are conscripted to fight the same war.

The nature of our profession is a team effort. That is why our occasional social events are key to life-work balance and self-care.

Celebration of community is key to establishing a sense of common purpose and culture of caring for colleagues as well as patients. When we gather outside of our workplace, we laugh together, we share insights and concerns; and by this we are encouraged. That is, we would say, the embers of our waning fires are fanned. You might say your internal batteries are recharged. The proof is that we are then able to *press on* for one more day.

So, there's your prescription: rest and recharge. As nurses, we know all too well that life is precious. So, work diligently, rest, and recharge.

**Q:** What is most important in the nursing profession?
**A:** That depends how one measures *important.* Some people would say, success is most important. But I beg to differ. To succeed is not the goal. The goal is to *serve* and if you serve well, you will succeed, no matter what your profession!

I would advise to begin with the end in mind. Know where you plan to be in five years, ten years. Dream big!

**Q:** Is there a way to bring more heart, soul, and healing into nursing in the 21st century?
**A:** The only way is the selfless way.

To illustrate, imagine you are in need of some kind of gear to move a precious, albeit heavy object. You find a piece of twine with one or two feeble strands. No, that won't do; it breaks apart with a little tug. So, you find the materials to weave together a thicker strand. You might begin with the cord of kindness, next to a cord of intelligence; add in a cord of technology, of caring, and a thick strand of humor. Braid them all together and voila! You have changed your workplace culture into a place you look forward to visiting each day.

That is the way to bring more heart, soul, and healing into the 21st century.

**Q:** How do you define the art of the Nursing Profession?
**A:** The art of nursing is the heart of nursing, tempered with the science that helps us help others. Of course, the science may produce magical new gadgets that give us insights into problems, but without the heart of caring, the science means nothing.

We should remember, there are no small works in service to others. All is opportunity and it all matters.

**Q:** Should Nurses Go Solo?
**A:** In general, I support a nurse's practice to the full extent that the law allows. In any case, the thing to avoid is pride, for as we all know, pride goes before a fall. In solo-provider nursing, pride may prevent you from referring a patient out to a physician, or perhaps you make the referral, just not expediently. We must still retain our checks and balances within any system.

**Q:** What about the illness you suffered after the Crimean War? How did that affect your daily life?
**A:** When I became ill in Turkey, the diagnosis was difficult. They called it Crimean Fever, but the causative agent was likely Brucellosis, as I've mentioned. I suffered for the rest of my life with it, over 50 years. The sciatica pain, plus the headaches, body aches, and occasional fever. Excruciating!

Today, the diagnostic pathology would be easily discovered and spit-spot, treated with antibiotics, of that we can be sure. Alas, the symptoms waxed and waned, and slowed me down completely at times.

But I must confess, if I weren't having such a cracking good time in heaven, there is one matter that would have me *rolling in my grave.* Upon my return from the war, some critics labeled my refusal to take part in the social world of my class, and my preference to shun the limelight, as *bouts of seclusion,* supposedly the result of depression or *lunacy*. Augh. Some people will concoct anything to sell more newspapers, I believe.

Now I ask you, as healthcare professionals, have you ever known a patient who experiences severe and continual pain, who does not suffer from bouts of depression?

Adjusting to a certain loss of mobility and independence is something every aged person must face, but I was semi-invalid in my late 30's.

'Twas a bitter pill to swallow, to say the least. Truth be told, it was necessary to reserve my strength for the battles that needed to be fought from my rooms!

I enjoyed the company of those whom I wished to see, in privacy. But I had no time, nor interest, in those who pandered to the hyperbolic tastes of socialites, unless it was for a great purpose.

Furthermore, humbly taken in perspective of the work I *did* accomplish in the next forty-odd *years, in my rooms*, bypassing social nonsense, leads one to critically reason by posing these questions:

- Would a lunatic have produced the same results?
- Could one who is incompetent write the volumes that oozed forth from my pen?

My ubiquitous detractors might have asked the Director of the School of Nursing at St. Thomas' regarding their ingenious suppositions about my mental state.

Perhaps, had they inquired at the Bureau of Internal Affairs in India, or the laying-in hospitals of Britain and Europe, they would have been obliged to receive other intelligence.

Had I not been lauded as an early practitioner of systems management, which you now know as *evidence-based health care?*

They could jolly well have asked at the War Office, if my comprehensive report on reform of the Army Hospital System was regarded as statistical nonsense from a perverted mind? Oh, I do become rather red-faced to recall it. I must continually remember to forgive them their chicanery.

Some slandered me as *ruthless* and *ambitious*! If that were so, what was I ruthless *about*? What were my ambitions? I sought no position. I took no remuneration. Thankfully, I had no need of it. This allowed me freedom to state my sincere convictions, and for that I have oft been the victim of slanderous and disingenuous gossip. I had seen the Army suffer, and that is where my heart lay, to reform the treatment of the British soldier.

Post-Crimea, the only position I held was as Director of the Nightingale Fund, an unpaid post, as were the two posts I held before and during the Crimean War.

Indeed, my consulting work, with the Viceroy and other decision-makers in India and other countries, cost me dearly of the coin of the realm, don't you know, not to mention an enormous effort, for I never had a patron nor a staff. I paid for my assistant's wages, the printing of my books, documents, etc., all on my own. My ambition was to save lives; my enemy, unnecessary mortality from disease. The terms *ruthless and ambitious* seem more suitable for dictators, warlords, and serial killers than for a nurse on a relentless campaign for clean air and water, decent food and housing for the poor, free education, honorable work, and safe childbirth for women!

Ah, but this is nothing new. We live in a fallen world. Do any good deed, and there will always be those who react with malice. Such behavior is a reflection of the nature of whom they serve, ergo themselves, which know is sinful. Unless we serve God, we serve the devil. Period.

Now, you've stirred me up. Please hear my rebuttal to a similar charge frequent in the secondary literature, especially by women historians, was that I had a 'low' opinion of women and I exploited them?!

Many who portrayed me as *anti-woman* refer to my 1861 letter to a friend, Mary Clarke Mohl[18], where I mentioned that women had given me no sympathy. I was actually replying to an argument Mary had made in her book on Mme Récamier. I told her that I had not found one woman who had altered her life one iota for me or my opinions, and then I mentioned eight men who had![17]

That was indeed the case in 1861, for not one of the women who nursed with me in the Crimean War continued to work with me afterwards. There was some dissention in the ranks, I can tell you. Some of the less dedicated nurses became involved with the soldiers, and some got themselves into, shall we say, *compromising circumstances*. That is all I will discuss on the subject; anything more would be indelicate.

On a happier note, the school in St Thomas' hospital opened in June 1860. The first significant advances made by my former pupils were when Agnes Jones became Superintendent of Nursing at the Liverpool Workhouse Infirmary. That was a great first! I mentored many such women, as is clear in numerous letters to me from former pupils as they went on to matronships around the world.

I also mentored women who sought my help who had not been trained in the Nightingale School, such as Eva Lückes at the Royal London Hospital and Ella Pirrie of Workhouse Infirmary in Belfast. It was my honor and pleasure to mentor many American, European, and Canadian nurses, as well as women in related fields such as Jane Senior, the first woman Poor Law inspector. But in 1861, none of this was evident.

If you check the sources, however, you would learn that I continued to give my time (and money) for years after. I actively mentored several 'workhouse infirmary' matrons. The triumph there was that I lived to see professional nursing established in a number of them, with full training schools.

While we're on the subject of errata, it has been stated that I *assisted* my friends John Stuart Mill, Charles Dickens, and Louisa Twining, in the Association for Improving Workhouse Infirmaries. I must humbly correct this error. I was the *instigator* who wrote and advocated for their help to take a stronger position on reform!

This came about because I was disappointed with the half measures legislated by the Metropolitan Poor Law Act in 1867, which *enabled* improved nursing, but did not *require* it. That was a blow, and I may have been downhearted for a day or so, but I went right to prayer and received the reminder from the Holy Spirit that this was a mere battle, not to be won easily, and that His Right was on our side! I did what I could do, as His providence opened up various opportunities to advocate.

Here I must speak to the other premise: that I was motivated by the urge for power and that there was evidence to support it. Well, that was pure poppycock, notwithstanding such "evidence" did not stand up to empirical scrutiny.

Oh! I had forgotten about the slings and arrows of outrageous dithering one must encounter here on this terrestrial ball. Please forgive my being taken-in by such remembrances. Let me pause to take my own advice, and breeeeeathe.

**Q:** If you were an American citizen, whom would you have voted for in the last election? **A:** Alas, I could not say. But if by asking this question, you mean to indicate the frustration you feel by the so-called *lame-duck congress,* you're not alone.

And I believe I have a simple solution: In the name of her majesty the Queen, I abjure you. Put down this notion of rebellion and re-join the Motherland!

**Q:** Do you have any concluding remarks?
**A:** Ah, yes, thank you for asking. There are a few thoughts I'd like to leave you, by way of application, regarding past, present, and future of nursing and healthcare.

About the present: Based upon what I've shared with you today, you may have already deduced: the problems you perceive now in nursing and healthcare are simply a variation of the same problems that have been common all along personally and system-wide.

From a systems point of view, we have too much work and not enough help or funds to carry it through. In other words, the healthcare system is broken. Why is it broken? All systems, being devices made by humans, are prone to two internal faults:1) They are imperfect and 2) They are in a continual state of flux. Any parent with a new baby will relate to this. Just when you think you have the bedtime down to a bit of a time schedule, another growth spurt occurs, a molar erupts, there's always something that wants our constant attention, and that interrupts our preconceived notion of what we think should take place. You must ride the waves like ships. (Perhaps today's metaphor might better be *surfers*?)

The healthcare paradigm of yesteryear will morph into the paradigm of the future.

As leaders, your job is to keep your eyes and ears open and speak up to those who have the power to make changes, as needs are known. Some of you are talented writers, some love research, and a few, like myself, thrill at the magic of statistical illustration. Some of you might even want to become a people's representative! Use your gifts!

And the future, what will it be? It's time for us to take action to help prevent the pain in this world.

Clearly, my time is up. So, if it's not to be me, then it must be ... YOU!

I would like to leave you all with this remembrance:
Seize the day and press on, with kindness.

Receive a discount when you share *Channeling Florence Nightingale* with your friends and colleagues!
Call 800-407-1688

# ODE TO THE CAREGIVERS

(In response to the question:
What encouragement would Miss Nightingale
give to nurses today?)

For those who strive to loosen the shackles
of academic rigor,
For the overworked and under-
nourished   late-night pizza connoisseur,
For the elderly and obsolete,
For the barefoot youth still pink of cheek,
For the brave who battle with weapons of
words,
Whose policy disarmaments go unheard,
For all who dream...
Press on.

This is for all those who wear caps,
And those who toil without them,
For those who hold-down two jobs,
Whose sobs are reflected in Kindle's glow,
Who sit on the bed, sing hymns, and listen
To snowflakes' fall and streetlights' glisten,
Whose bravery yet is still unsung,
This is for you:
Connect with your team,
And press on.

This is for all who think you're no hero,
A zero,
You marshal courage to give it your best,
Whose life at work is a war zone
Or in your home,

You *invest* in others more than your IRAs.
Those who aim for artistry in life,
Not strife,
Press on.

Press on as you sort it out,
Press on as you grieve the voices,
Press on with the lump in your throat,
When you hear the world rejoices,
And listen
To what's missing.
Press on.

For those who are balding, worn, and weak,
Carrying on through personal hell,
There is one whose help you can seek,
Ring God's bell!
And when the news begs a witness,
Speak what you know in this,
Don't just whistle Vivaldi,
Press on.

For those whose blood pumps more than
Five liters a minute,
Go ahead, begin it!
Altho' life's poem may seem like cacophony,
One day you will hear the symphony.
For now, hitch your star to starting over.
Press on.

And finally, I'll dream out loud.
Press on and make me proud
That my life's poem meant more than a
riddle to you.
This guru will reckon some winging alone.

Yes, your voice is small,
But keep singing!
Press on.
Press on.
Oh, for the love of God
And for the children,
Press on

# FOOTNOTES

Preface

[1] *'Whatever Happened to My Paradigm?'* was created for a nursing conference.
*'Full Frontal Nursing: A Comedy With Dark Spots'* was featured on the list of 'Ones to Watch' from *Backstage West Magazine* during the San Francisco Fringe Theatre Festival, garnered *thumbs up* reviews, and had a subsequent run in San Francisco.

Act I Scene I - Integrity

[2] Cameron, J., *The Artist's Way*, 1992
Scene ii

[3] Rom 8:28
[4] Shomer, E., Twelve Rooms of the Nile
[5] I Cor. 7:8

Act II Scene I – Insight

[6] The result was a film script, *Walking Point,* which tells the fictional story of a nurse who enlists in the Army because she wants to see Europe, then gets sent unwillingly to Vietnam. Once there, she finds the love of her life, loses him as a casualty of war, and nineteen years later, learns he never really died.

Everything else is based on the true remembrances of the host of veterans I interviewed. (The novel based on the script is in process.)

Scene ii
[7] As You Like It, Act II, vii

Act 3 Scene i - Innovation
[8] Viereck, G.S., interview with Einstein, 1929
[9] Nightingale, F., *Cassandra,* 1852
[10] Norman, E., *We Band of Angels*, 1999

Q&A
[11] Nightingale, F., *Notes on Hospitals*, 1863
[12] Nightingale, F., Sick Nursing and Health Nursing,
[13] Nightingale, F., (Calabria & Macrae, Ed.), Suggestions for Thought by Florence Nightingale: Selections and Commentaries, 1994
[14] Nightingale, F., *Notes on Hospitals*, 1863
[15] Nightingale, F., (Calabria & Macrae, Ed.), Suggestions for Thought by Florence Nightingale: Selections and Commentaries, 1994
[16] Ibid
[17] Prov. 25:22
[18] Nightingale, F. (Vicinus & Nergaard), Ever Yours, Florence Nightingale: Selected Letters, 1984

# Florence Nightingale Timeline

- (May 12, 1820) – Born in Florence, Italy
- (1837)First "call from God"
- (1837-39) Nightingale family tours Europe
- (1847-48) Travels to Italy, attends retreat at the convent Trinità dei Monti
- (1849-50) Travels to Egypt, (hears her second "call from God,") and to Greece. Visits Kaiserswerth, in Germany, on the return home
- (1851)Attends Kaiserswerth Deaconess Mutterhaus for three months nurses training course (passed exam), begins writing treatise on religion and spirituality
- (1852) Considers conversion to Roman Catholicism
- (1853) Appointment as Superintendent of the Institution for the Care of Sick Gentlewomen in Distressed Circumstances in Harley Street, London
- (1854-1856) Appointed Superintendent of Nurses in the British army hospitals of the Crimea conflict
- (1857) Influences the establishment of the Royal Commission on the Health of the British Army
- (1858) Completes Notes on Matters Affecting the Health, Efficiency and Hospital Administration of the British Army
- (1859) Publishes *Notes on Hospitals;* influences the establishment of the Royal

Commission on the Health of the British Army in India

- (1860) Completes *Notes on Nursing, What it is and What it is Not;* writes curriculum and oversees establishment of the Nightingale Training School for Nurses, St. Thomas' Hospital, London; publishes *Suggestions for Thought*
- (1861) Oversees the establishment of Kings College Training school for Midwives; receives request for assistance by the US Secretary of War to organize army hospitals for casualties during the American Civil War
- (1863) Published articles on The Contagious Diseases Act; Observations on the evidence contained in data for the Royal Commission on the Sanitary State of the Army in India; How People May Live and Not Die in India
- (1864) Publishes Suggestions in regard to Sanitary Works required for the Improvement of Indian Stations
- (1865) Publishes Suggestions on a system of nursing for hospitals in India
- (1867) Organizes the Office of Sanitary Commission of India; Publishes Suggestions on the subject of providing training, and organizing nurses for the sick poor in workhouse infirmaries
- (1868) Publishes Method of improving the nursing service of hospitals
- (1870) Advisor to French and Prussian army medical service during Franco-Prussian War; Supervises activities for the *National Society for Aid to the Sick and Wounded*
- (1871) Publishes Introductory notes on lying-in institutions

- (1872) Assists friend Benjamin Jowitt to translate Plato's works into English; formats plan for *Children's Bible*
- (1873) Fraser's magazine publishes her two articles on theological subjects; writes *Notes From Devotional Authors of the Middle Ages*
- (1874) Father, W.E. Nightingale, dies
- (1880) Mother, Francis Nightingale, dies
- (1882) Organizes team of nurses to serve during Anglo-Egyptian War
- (1887) Queen Victoria's Golden Jubilee; Florence celebrates her Jubilee (i.e.,50 years after her calling from God)
- (1890) Sister, Parthenope, dies
- (1894) Parthenope's husband, Sir Harry Varney, dies
- (1907) *Order of Merit* from King Edward VII
- (1910) Age 90, dies

# REFERENCES

Bostridge, M. (2008). *Florence Nightingale: The Making of an Icon*. New York: Farrar Straus and Giroux.

Cook, E. T. (1913). *The Life of Florence Nightingale*. London: Macmillan and Co.

Dossey, B. M. (2010). *Florence Nightingale: Mystic, Visionary, Healer*. Philadelphia Pa.: F.A. Davis Co.

McDonald, L., Ed. (2001–). *The Collected Works of Florence Nightingale.* (vol. 1-13) Waterloo, Ont.: Wilfrid Laurier University Press

Nightingale, F. (1992). *Cassandra and Other Selections from Suggestions for Thought* (M. Poovey, Ed.). New York: New York University Press.

Nightingale, F. (1990). *Ever Yours, Florence Nightingale: Selected Letters* (M. Vicinus and B. Nergaard, Eds.). Cambridge MA: Harvard University Press.

Nightingale, F.(Keele, M. Ed.), (1981). *Florence Nightingale in Rome: Letters Written by Florence Nightingale in Rome in the winter of 1847-1848* Philadelphia: American Philosophical Society.

Nightingale, F. (M. Calabria, Ed.),(1997). *Florence Nightingale in Egypt and Greece: Her Diary and "Visions"* Albany: State University of New York Press.

Nightingale, F. (S. Goldie, Ed.),(1997). *Letters from the Crimea, 1854–1856* New York: Mandolin.

Nightingale, F. (A. Sattin, Ed.),(1987). *Letters from Egypt: A Journey on the Nile 1849–50*. London: Barrie and Jenkins.

Nightingale, F. (2008). *Notes on Nursing and Other Writings*. New York: Kaplan Publishing.

Nightingale, F. (M. Calabria and J. Macrae, Eds.), (1994). *Suggestions for Thought by Florence Nightingale: Selections and Commentaries.* Philadelphia: University of Pennsylvania Press.

Rosenberg, C., Ed. (1989). *Florence Nightingale on Hospital Reform*. New York: Garland Publishing, Inc.

Webb, V. (2002). *Florence Nightingale: The Making of a Radical Theologian*. St. Louis, MO: Chalice Press.

# Acknowledgements

EVERYONE KNOWS A CREATIVE PROJECT doesn't hatch by itself. There were many people responsible for the care and nurturing of the seed of an idea that grew and finally burst forth into a staged performance, and now, the book.

I'd like to thank many of my National Speakers Association friends (as inspiring bunch if ever there was one), who continue to function as laboratory partners. They helped me poke and prod and examine various concepts that fuel the *passion to share a message*. In particular, I'd like to thank Barry Wishner for the challenge and the faith he offered, to believe I could do this historical icon justice, especially when I came up with excuses why I didn't have time to invest in this project. There are so many other NSA folks who have helped me through the details of putting this together. Michael Soon Lee, Roberta Guise, Jim Carrillo, to name a few.

Bobby Weinapple, ever an inspirational creative director and friend, gave sage input to hone the script and helped stage the first performance.

Karen Willis finished major portions of the transcription, Amanda Rosenblatt and Keith Carlson helped edit, Jim Carrillo and Mary Esther Loranger assisted with the taping of the video promo blogs, and Cindy Hadden attended to whatever else needed to be done. I'm blessed to call you all friends.

I'm grateful also to several celebrated authors and many helpful friends who contributed their time to review the manuscript and give encouragement and advice. I must also mention all the people who enjoyed the live show and encouraged me to "make a book of this!"

I'm thankful for my prayer partners, past and present, who lift me up when I feel overwhelmed. They remind me that no matter the roadblocks, the greater good will be served when you use your gifts in service.

On the home front, I appreciate that throughout the years, my now three grown children have been supportive and proud of their mom's many creative projects that sometime caused me to keep crazy hours and travel a lot. They are my joy and continual inspiration.

Today, I'm pleased to report that since the first edition of this book, the character portrayal of Miss Nightingale has delighted audiences in many parts of the US and three other countries. Audiences requested I add the photos of the show, hence the enhanced version you hold. Other news is that in 2020, our team is looking forward to the extended tour and celebrations of the 200th anniversary of her birth.

With great appreciation
Candy Campbell
3rd edition, March 2019

# SUGGESTIONS ON HOW TO USE THIS BOOK

**Bring the CATEGORY OF ONE to your event!**

**Conference Keynote:**

Dr. Campbell's *Channeling Florence Nightingale* presentation is an edutaining and thought-provoking kick-off or conclusion for your conference.

This high-energy program will invigorate participants to reframe their practice to face the future of healthcare with a spirit of fellowship, confidence, and creativity. Audience members relish the idea of interacting with Miss Nightingale during the extemporaneous Q&A session.

**Team Workshops:**

As a doctoral prepared researcher, clinician, educator, and professional actor/director with years of stand-up and improv comedy experience, Dr. Candy Campbell also provides interactive, intensive, workshop/breakout sessions.

The key?

She invokes the modern Miss Nightingale's suggested communication facilitation, applied theatrical exercises (AIEs).

Participants say these workshops are effective, affordable and FUN. Interprofessional students learn skills that result in heightened ability to quickly form trusting alliances, spontaneously adapt to unforeseen situations, critically communicate, and problem solve.

## Leadership Retreats:

Your leadership team will benefit from FUN and powerful train-the-trainer educational method of communication techniques that lead to maximum silo-breaking and patient satisfaction.

## Caregiver Retreats:

Available as half-day and full-day sessions, this program honors the legacy of the healing professions, and provides practical interprofessional communication tools for non-professional caregivers that facilitate conflict resolution and confidence for speaking up.

## Recognition Events:

Much more than a motivational pep rally, the modern *Miss Nightingale* shares practical and proven strategies for personal and professional success.

# About the Author

Dr. Candy Campbell is an award-winning actress, author, filmmaker, and fine artist.

To create this character portrayal, Dr. Campbell read most of Nightingale's 200 books and many of her 15,000 letters. In the process, she was invited to be a member of the esteemed Nightingale Society of academic historians.

As a professional actor, when she is not performing onstage or in commercials, Campbell works with corporate and individual clients to achieve peak performance cultures. This includes giving keynotes and leading workshops on leadership, team building, and presentation skills, with the use of applied experiential exercises from the arts.

In the early 1990's, Campbell co-founded an improv and stand-up comedy group, The Barely Insane Players, which eventually led to three solo shows, "Whatever Happened to My Paradigm," "Full-Frontal Nursing: A Comedy With Dark Spots," and the iconic, "Channeling Florence Nightingale: Integrity, Insight, Innovation."

Her background in healthcare includes many years of clinical, professorial, and administrative posts. As a healthcare policy advocate, Candy has appeared on many media networks, speaking about various topics. Her articles on interprofessional communication and clinical health issues have appeared in online and peer-reviewed publications. She is also a legal nurse consultant.

Her personal story of resilience, despite rape trauma, inspired her work and research about PTSD with healthcare persons who are Vietnam Veterans and later with families of premature babies. The results became a film script, Walking Point, and a documentary film, *Micropremature Babies: How Low Can You Go?*

The ability to imagine herself in someone else's skin has served her well personally and professionally.

For more information:
visit candycampbell.com
call 800-407-1688
or email
candy@candycampbell.com

# OTHER BOOKS BY CANDY CAMPBELL

- *Improv to Improve Healthcare: A System for Creative Problem-Solving*
- *My Mom Is A Nurse*
- *My Grandma Is A Nurse*
- *Mi Mama Es Una Enfermera*
- *Good Things Come In Small Packages: I Was A Preemie*

AWARD-WINNING DOCUMENTARY FILM:

- *Micropremature Babies: How Low Can You Go?*

Made in the USA
Monee, IL
24 September 2021